It was a bad day for Kim and Sam.

1

They had a lot of sums to do for Miss Mills.

Kim hid Sam's pen and he got mad.

"Go and do your sums in the school hall," said Miss Mills.

'Look, Sam!" said Kim. "The school hall is all wet!"

"One of the taps is on!" said Sam.

"Let's mop it up," said Kim.

"Kim! You are all wet!" said Sam.

'**You** are all wet, too!" said Kim.

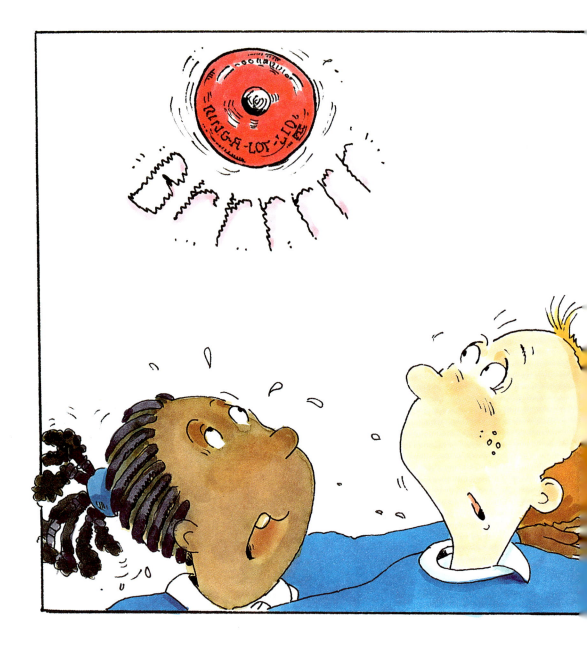

"Oh no!" said Sam. "That's the bell!"

Oh no!" said Kim. "Miss Mills will tell us off!"

"Come on, let's mop it up!" said Sam.

"Sam and Kim!" said Miss Mills. "You are all wet!"

"One of the taps was on, Miss Mills," said Sam and Kim.

'Did you mop it up?" said Miss Mills.
'Yes!" said Sam and Kim.

"Thank you! Now you can do your sums!" said Miss Mills.

"Yes, Miss Mills," said Sam and Kim.